Nina's Clippings

Nina had a large collection of poetry and articles. These "Clippings" are from her collection.

Compiled by
C. V. Kirkstadt

Published by CVKPress, Loveland, Colorado

ISBN 978-0-9982088-2-4

In Memory of

Nina Kirkstadt

Table of Contents

About Nina

Nina was born May 22, 1914 in Fremont, Ohio, the fifth of ten children. Her parents were Adrian Meyer and Florence Castle. When she was 14 her mother died. Her father was unable to keep the large family together. When the family was split up, Nina was sent to live with an Aunt and Uncle in Cleveland, Ohio. Nina married Harold Kirkstadt on June 10, 1936. They had two children, James (Jim) and Carol. They lived in Cleveland Heights, Ohio. Nina was active in the Parent Teachers Association (PTA) and her Church. In 1988 Nina and Harold moved to Johnstown, Pennsylvania to be near Jim and his family. Toward the end of her life, Nina suffered from osteoporosis and irritation of the throat. Despite these difficulties she was always cheerful and uncomplaining.

Some of the poems in this collection were used in correspondence with family and friends. You will find samples of Nina's handwriting included. Nina was born left handed...in school she was forced to write with her right hand. Her beautiful penmanship was an example of her determination to do her best at whatever she did.

Nina felt strongly about living a good life, she frequently would give advice in the form of a story, saying "I once knew someone who did .... and the result was ....". We were expected to take the hint.

When my brother, Jim and I were children, Mother frequently read stories and poetry to us. The section "When we were small" includes some favorites.

I remember my Mother as always encouraging and supportive. She had a strong faith in a loving God. She showed, by example, the Christian principles that guided her life. She approached life with energy and enthusiasm.

I hope this collection will inspire all who read it.
C. V. Kirkstadt
December 2004

I met God in the morning
When the day was at its best,
And His Presence came like sunrise,
Like a glory within my breast.

All day long the Presence lingered,
All day long He stayed with me;
And we sailed in perfect calmness
O're a very troubled sea.

Other ships were blown and battered,
Other ships were sore distressed;
But the winds that seemed to drive them,
Brought to me a peace and rest.

Then I thought of other mornings,
With a keen remorse of mind,
When I too, had loosed the moorings,
With the Presence left behind.

So I think I know the secret
Learned from many a troubled way;
You must seek God in the morning
If you want Him through the day!

Bishop Ralph S. Cushman

The morning light is breaking Lord,
Another day is here.
Life's problems must again be met
With heart and vision clear.

Strength for today I ask, Dear Lord,
Strength only for today.
Renew my faith, my hope revive
Illumine my skies of gray.

For yesterday is past, dear Lord,
Tomorrow I ne'er may see,
Today alone lies in my grasp
To use or lose for eternity.

Help me lend a helping hand,
To dry the falling tears,
To give to all whose lives touch mine
Some comfort or good cheer.

Help me link my poor weak self
With its longings hopes and fears,
In service to my fellow man
Battling through this vale of tears.

Just for today, day by day
Courage and strength I pray.
Garnering the good, forgiving the wrong
Tell I've lived my last today.

Author unknown

sent to Nina from her brother, Clarence
December 1980

Rules for Daily Living

Begin the day with God
    Kneel down to Him in prayer;
    Lift up your heart to His abode,
    And seek His love to share.

Open the Book of God
    And read a portion there:
    That it might hallow all thy thoughts,
    And sweeten all thy care.

Go through the day with God,
    Whatever thy work may be,
    Wherever thou art, at home, abroad,
    He still is near to thee.

Converse in mind with God,
    Thy spirit heavenward raise:
    Acknowledge every good bestowed,
    And offer grateful praise.

Conclude the day with God,
    Thy sins to Him confess,
    Trust in the Lord's atoning blood,
    And plead His righteousness.

Lie down at night with God
    Who gives His servants sleep,
    And when thou tread'st the vale of death
    He will thee guard and keep.

Author unknown

THE BURDEN OF THE HOUR
George Klingle

God broke our years into hours and days,
That hour by hour, and day by day
Just going on a little way
We might be able all along,
To keep quite strong.

Should all the weight of life be laid
Across our shoulders at just one place,
And the future, rife with woe and struggle,
Meet us face to face;
We could not go;
Our feet would stop, and so
God lays a little on us every day.

And never, I believe in all life's way,
Will burdens bear so deep,
Or pathways lie so steep,
But we can go, if by God's power
We only bear the burden of the hour.

Power Shortage

Recently, excessive heat and humidity brought electric power cutbacks throughout five mid-Atlantic states and the District of Columbia. In mountainous areas how often has electric power been cut off because of trees falling on the lines or from excessive ice and snow!

We have become so accustomed to electric power in our homes, as well as for running elevators and vast industrial machines that we can hardly imagine what would happen if suddenly we were all denied electric power!

Some students of prophecy believe this could happen and that primitive weapons, such as bows and arrows may again be used (Ezekiel 39:9). However, regardless as to whether we may always have electrical power or not, how wonderful for the Christians to know that there will never be any lack of spiritual power!

When the Lord Jesus was upon earth, He said, *"All power is given unto me in heaven and in earth."* (Matthew 28:18) *"The gospel of Christ: for it is still the power of God unto salvation to everyone that believeth."* (Romans 1:16)

The sweet story of Christ's death for our sins and the resurrection for our justification has lost none of it's power or charm. The most sinful and the most self-righteous person can be saved through faith in Christ today, as of yore.

And the believer today is kept by the power of God (1 Peter 1:5), regardless of the number of trials he is called upon to pass through. Ephesians 3:20 tells us He *"is able to do exceeding abundantly above all that we ask or think, according to the power that worketh in us."* The power needed is available to us.

He is also able to strengthen us with all might according to His glorious power into all patience and long-suffering with joyfulness! (1 Corinthians 1:11)

One of these days the Lord will cease his longsuffering in regard to man's wickedness. He will judge the evil and He will take to Himself His great power and He will reign over the earth in righteousness (Revelation 11:17).

In the meantime, let us never fear the loss or shortage of power on the part of Him who is altogether lovely, altogether wise and altogether powerful.

Tom M. Olson

The light of God surrounds me
The love of God enfolds me
The power of God protects me
The presence of God watches over me
Where ever I am. God is.

Prayer by James Dillet Freeman

May the grace of our Lord Jesus Christ, which is sufficient;
The love of God our Heavenly Father, which is eternal;
And the comfort of the Holy Spirit, which is constant;
Be with us now and forever.

Amen

Consolation
Lilla M. Alexander

There is never a day so dreary
But God can make it bright,
And unto the soul that trusts Him
He giveth songs in the night.
There is never a path so hidden,
But God can lead the way.
If we seek the Spirit's guidance
And patiently wait and pray.

There is never a cross so heavy
But the nail-scarred hands are there,
Outstretched in tender compassion
The burden to help us bear.
There is never a heart so broken
But the loving Lord can heal,
The heart that was pierced on Calvary
Doth still for His loved ones feel.

There is never a life so darkened,
So hopeless and unblessed,
But may be filled with the light of God
And enter His promised rest.
There is never a sin or sorrow,
There is never a care or loss,
But that we may bring it to Jesus
And leave at the foot of the Cross.

A message for Today

" When the day is torn by trouble
And your heart is lone & sad,
Just remember all the blessings
And the good that you have had.
God's sure hand is ever leading;
Lift the curtain of despair.
For however deep life's shadow,
You will find your Father there.

There's a path His love is planning
Which must mean the best for you,
There are blessings, countless blessings,
Which are hidden now from view.
Tune your anxious heart to patience,
Walk by faith where sight is dim,
Loving God, be calm and trustful
And leave everything to Him.

Has not yesterday a lesson
Bearing on your present need?
" Daily bread for daily hunger "
Is the message there we read.
Thus our heart gains full assurance
That His love will be our stay.
Giving strength and help and blessing,
As we need them for today. "
     J. merok Chambers

If God should go on Strike
Walt Huntley

How good it is that God above has never gone on strike,
Because he was not treated fair in things he didn't like,
If only once he'd given up and said, "That's it, I'm through.
I've had enough of those on earth, so this is what I'll do. "

I'll give my orders to the sun .. "cut off the heat supply. "
And to the moon, "give no more light, and run the oceans dry."
Then just to make things really tough and put the pressure on,
"Turn off the vital oxygen 'till every breath is gone."

You know he would be justified, if fairness was the game,
For no one has been more abused or met with more disdain
Than God, and yet he carries on, supplying you and me
With all the favors of his grace, and everything for free.

Men say they want a better deal, and so on strike they go,
But what a deal we've given God to whom all things we owe.
We don't care whom we hurt, to gain the things we like;
But what a mess we'd all be in, if God should go on strike.

Whatever you read, though the page may allure,
Read nothing of which you are perfectly sure
Consternation at once would be seen in your look
If the Lord should say solemnly, "Show me that book"

Whatever you write, in haste or withheld,
Write nothing you would not like Jesus to read.
Whatever you sing in the midst of your glee,
Sing nothing that God's listening ear could displease.

Wherever you go, never go where you'd fear
God's asking the question, "What doest thou here?"
Whatever the pastime in which you engage,
For the cheering of youth or the solace of age,
Turn away from each pleasure
      you'd shrink from pursuing..
Were the Lord to look down and say,
      What are you doing?"

When you think, when you speak,
      when you read, when you write,
When you sing, when you walk, when you seek for delight.
To be kept from all evil at home or abroad,
Live always as under the eye of your God.

What ever you think, both in joy and in woe,
Think nothing you would not like Jesus to know,
Whatever you say in whisper or clear,
Say nothing you would not like Jesus to hear.

                              Author unknown

One Solitary Life
James A. Francis

He was born in an obscure village. He worked in a carpenter shop until he was thirty, and then for three years He was an itinerant preacher. He never wrote a book. He never held an office.

He never owned a home. He never traveled more than two hundred miles from the place where He was born. He had no credentials but Himself.

While still a young man, the tide of popular opinion turned against Him. His friends ran away. One of them denied Him. He was turned over to His enemies. He went through the mockery of a trial. He was nailed upon a cross between two thieves. When He was dead, He was taken down and laid in a borrowed grave through the kindness of a friend.

Nineteen wide centuries have come and gone, today He is the centerpiece of the human race. I am far within the mark when I say that all the armies that ever marched, and all the navies that ever were built, and all the parliaments that ever sat, and all the kings that ever reigned, put together, have not affected the life of man upon this earth as powerfully as that One Solitary Life.

THE BIBLE

I am the Bible
   I am God's wonderful library.
I am always, and above all, the truth.

To the weary pilgrim,
   I am a good, strong staff.
To the one who sits in gloom,
   I am the glorious light.

To those who stoop beneath heavy burdens,
   I am sweet rest.
To him who has lost his way,
   I am a safe guide.

To those who have been hurt by sin,
   I am healing balm.
To the discouraged,
   I whisper a glad message of hope.

To those who are distressed by the storms of life,
   I am an anchor sure and steadfast.
To those who suffer in lonely solitude,
   I am a cool soft hand resting
   upon a fevered brow.

Oh, child of man, to best defend me,
   just use me!

Author unknown

Jesus said to him, 'You shall love the Lord your God with all your heart, and with all your soul, and with all your mind.' This is the first and great commandment.

And the second is like it: 'You shall love your neighbor as yourself.' On these two commandments hang all the Law and the Prophets.

Matthew 22:37-40

And now, Israel, what does the Lord your God require of you, but to fear the Lord your God, to walk in all His ways and to love Him, to serve the Lord your God with all your heart and with all your soul, and to keep the commandments of the Lord and His statutes which I command you today for your good?

Deuteronomy 10:12-13

....but you shall love your neighbor as yourself ....

Leviticus 19:18b

Hear, O Israel: the Lord our God, the Lord is one!
You shall love the Lord your God with all your heart, and with all your soul, and with all your strength. And these words which I command you today shall be in your heart. You shall teach them diligently to your children, and shall talk of them when you sit in your house, when you walk by the way, when you lie down, and when you rise up.

Deuteronomy 6:4-7

He has shown you, O man, what is good; and what does the LORD require of you but to do justly, to love mercy, and to walk humbly with your God?

Micah 6:8

The Lord bless you and keep you;
The Lord make His face shine upon you,
    and be gracious to you;
The Lord lift up His countenance upon you,
    and give you peace.

Numbers 6:24-26

For I know that my Redeemer lives,
    and He shall stand at last on the earth;
And after my skin is destroyed, this I know,
    that in my flesh I shall see God,
Whom I shall see for myself,
    and my eyes shall behold, and not another.
How my heart yearns within me!

Job 19:25-27

You will keep him in perfect peace,
    whose mind is stayed on You,
        because he trusts in You.

Isaiah 26:3

Fear not, for I am with you;
    be not dismayed, for I am your God.
I will strengthen you, yes, I will help you,
    I will uphold you with My righteous right hand.

Isaiah 41:10

My son, give attention to my words;
    incline your ear to my sayings.
Do not let them depart from your eyes;
    keep them in the midst of your heart;
For they are life to those who find them,
    and health to all their flesh.

Proverbs 4:20-22

A Psalm of David (Psalm 23)

The Lord is my shepherd; I shall not want.
He makes me to lie down in green pastures;
He leads me beside the still waters.
He restores my soul;
He leads me in the paths of righteousness
for His name's sake.

Yea, though I walk through the valley
of the shadow of death,
I will fear no evil; for You are with me;
Your rod and Your staff, they comfort me.

You prepare a table before me
in the presence of my enemies;
You anoint my head with oil;
My cup runs over.
Surely goodness and mercy shall follow me
all the days of my life;
And I will dwell in the house of the Lord forever.

A Psalm of Thanksgiving (Psalm 100)

Make a joyful shout to the Lord, all you lands!
Serve the Lord with gladness;
come before His presence with singing.
Know that the Lord, He is God;
It is He who has made us, and not we ourselves;
We are His people, and the sheep of His pasture.
Enter into His gates with thanksgiving,
and into His courts with praise.
Be thankful unto Him, and bless His name.
For the Lord is good; His mercy is everlasting,
and His truth endures to all generations.

The heavens declare the glory of God;

Psalm 19:1a

Let the words of my mouth
and the meditation of my heart
be acceptable in Your sight,
O Lord, my strength, and my redeemer.

Psalm 19:14

The steps of a good man are ordered by the Lord,
and He delights in his way.

Psalm 37:23

God is our refuge and strength,
a very present help in trouble.

Psalm 46:1

Create in me a clean heart, O God,
and renew a steadfast spirit within me.

Psalm 51:10

But it is good for me to draw near to God;
I have put my trust in the Lord God,
that I may declare all Your works.

Psalm 73:28

I will lift up mine eyes unto the hills ...
from whence comes my help?
My help comes from the Lord,
who made heaven and earth.

Psalm 121:1-2

Ask, and it will be given to you;
Seek, and you will find;
Knock, and it will be opened to you.

Matthew 7:7 & Luke 11:9

Therefore I say to you, whatever things you ask when you pray, believe that you receive them, and you will have them.

Mark 11:24

You are the light of the world. A city that is set on a hill cannot be hidden. Nor do they light a lamp, and put it under a basket, but on a lampstand; and it gives light to all who are in the house. Let your light so shine before men, that they may see your good works and glorify your Father in heaven.

Matthew 5:14-16

But seek first the kingdom of God,
    and His righteousness,
        and all these things shall be added to you.

Matthew 6:33

For where your treasure is,
    there your heart will be also.

Matthew 6:21 & Luke 12:34

And Jesus increased in wisdom and stature,
    and in favor with God and men.

Luke 2:52

Whoever comes to Me, and hears My sayings and does them, I will show you whom he is like:

He is like a man building a house, who dug deep and laid the foundation on the rock. And when the flood arose, and the stream beat vehemently against that house, and could not shake it, for it was founded on the rock.

But he who heard and did nothing is like a man who built a house on the earth without a foundation, against which the stream beat vehemently; and immediately it fell. And the ruin of that house was great.

Luke 6:47-49

For God so loved the world, that He gave His only begotten Son, that whoever believes in Him should not perish, but have everlasting life.

John 3:16

A new commandment I give to you, that you love one another; as I have loved you, that you also love one another. By this all will know that you are My disciples, if you have love for one another.

John 13:34-35

Let not your heart be troubled; you believe in God, believe also in Me. In My Father's house are many mansions; if it were not so, I would have told you. I go to prepare a place for you. And if I go and prepare a place for you, I will come again and receive you to Myself; that where I am, there you may be also. And where I go you know, and the way you know.

John 14:1-4

Jesus said to him, "I am the way, the truth, and the life. No one comes to the Father except through Me."

John 14:6

But the Helper, the Holy Spirit, whom the Father will send in My name, He will teach you all things, and bring to your remembrance all things that I said to you.

John 14:26

But the fruit of the Spirit is love, joy, peace, long-suffering, kindness, goodness, faithfulness, gentleness, self-control. Against such there is no law.

Galatians 5:22-23

And we know that all things work together for good to those who love God, to those who are the called according to His purpose.

Romans 8:28

I beseech you therefore, brethren, by the mercies of God, that you present your bodies a living sacrifice, holy, acceptable to God, which is your reasonable service. And do not be conformed to this world, but be transformed by the renewing of your mind, that you may prove what is that good and acceptable and perfect will of God.

Romans 12:1-2

Finally, brethren, whatever things are true, whatever things are noble, whatever things are just, whatever things are pure, whatever things are lovely, whatever things are of good report, if there is any virtue and if there is anything praiseworthy — meditate on these things.
The things which you learned and received and heard and saw in me, these do, and the God of peace will be with you.

Philippians 4:8-9

But without faith it is impossible to please Him, for he who comes to God must believe that He is, and that He is a rewarder of those who diligently seek Him.

Hebrews 11:6

Or do you not know that your body is the temple of the Holy Spirit who is in you, whom you have from God, and you are not your own? For you were bought at a price; therefore glorify God in your body and in your spirit, which are God's.

1 Corinthians 6:19

Therefore, whether you eat or drink, or whatever you do, do all to the glory of God.

1 Corinthians 10:31

Love suffers long and is kind; love does not envy; love does not parade itself, is not puffed up; does not behave rudely, does not seek its own, is not provoked, thinks no evil; does not rejoice in iniquity but rejoices in the truth; bears all things, believes all things, hopes all things, endures all things. Love never fails.

1 Corinthians 13:4-8a

Thus also faith by itself, if it does not have works, is dead.

James 2:17

All Scripture is given by inspiration of God, and is profitable for doctrine, for reproof, for correction, for instruction in righteousness, that the man of God may be complete, thoroughly equipped for every good work.

2 Timothy 3:16-17

And God shall wipe away every tear from their eyes; there shall be no more death, nor sorrow, nor crying. There shall be no more pain, for the former things have passed away.

Revelation 21:4

A Psalm of Life

Henry Wadsworth Longfellow

Tell me not, in mournful numbers,
  Life is but an empty dream!
For the soul is dead that slumbers,
  And things are not what they seem.

Life is real! Life is earnest!
  And the grave is not its goal;
Dust thou art, to dust returnest,
  Was not spoken of the soul.

Not enjoyment, and not sorrow,
  Is our destined end or way;
But to act, that each tomorrow
  Find us farther than today.

Art is long, and Time is fleeting,
  And our hearts, though stout and brave,
Still, like muffled drums, and beating
  Funeral marches to the grave.

In the world's broad field of battle,
  In the bivouac of life,
Be not like dumb, driven cattle!
  Be a hero in the strife!

Trust no Future, howe'er pleasant!
  Let the dead Past bury its dead!
  Act, — act in the living Present!
Heart within, and God o'erhead!

Lives of great men all remind us
  We can make our lives sublime,
And, departing, leave behind us
  Footprints on the sands of time.

Footprints, that perhaps another,
  Sailing o'er life's solemn main,
A forlorn and shipwrecked brother,
  Seeing, shall take heart again.

Let us then be up and doing,
  With a heart for any fate;
Still achieving, still pursuing,
  Learn to labor and to wait.

WHAT I LIVE FOR

Nina's mother's favorite poem

I live for those who love me,
    Whose hearts are kind and true;
For the heaven that smiles above me,
    And awaits my coming too;
For all human ties that bind me,
For the task by God assigned me,
For the bright hopes yet to find me,
    And the good that I can do.

I live to learn their story
    Who suffered for my sake;
To emulate their glory,
    And follow in their wake:
Bards, patriots, martyrs, sages,
The heroic of all ages,
Whose deeds crowd History's pages
    And Time's great volume.

I live to hold communion
    With all that is divine;
To feel there is a union
    'Twixt nature's heart and mine;
To profit by affliction,
Reap truth from fields of fiction,
Grow wiser by conviction,
    And fulfill God's grand design.

I live to hail that season
    By gifted ones foretold,
When men shall live by reason,
    And not alone by gold;
When man to man united,
And every wrong thing righted,
The whole world shall be lighted,
    As Eden was of old.

I live for those who love me,
    For those who know me true;
For the heaven that smiles above me,
    And awaits my coming too;
For the cause that lacks assistance,
For the wrong that needs assistance,
For the future in the distance,
    And the good that I can do.

        GEORGE LENNAEUS BANKS

Dear God,

Help me to be a sport in this game of life.
I don't ask for any place in the line-up;
Play me where you need me.

I only ask for the stuff to give you
One hundred percent of what I've got.

If all the hard drives come my way,
I thank you for the compliment.
Help me to take the bad breaks as part of the game.

And God, help me always to play on the square,
No matter what the other players do
Help me to see that often the best part of the game
Is helping the other guy.

Finally, God, if fate seems to uppercut me,
And I'm laid up in sickness or injury,
Help me to accept that as part of the game also
Help me not to whimper or squawk,
Or complain that I had a raw deal.

When in the dusk I hear the final gun,
I ask for no great honors or compliments.
I only want to know that you are pleased
And that the game has been Yours.

Amen

                                    Author unknown

Compensation
Edgar A. Guest

I'd like to think when life is done
That I had filled a needed post.
That here and there I'd paid my fare
With more than idle talk and boast;

That I had taken gifts divine
The breath of life and manhood fine,
And tried to use them now and then
In service for my fellow men.

I'd hate to think when life is through,
That I had lived my round of years
A useless kind that leaves behind
No record in this vale of tears;

That I had wasted all my days,
By trading only selfish ways.
And that this world would be the same,
If it had never known my name.

I'd like to think, when life is done,
That here and there, there shall remain
A happier spot that might have not
Existed, had I toiled for gain.

That someone's cheery voice and smile
Shall prove that I had been worthwhile.
That I had paid with something fine
My debt to God for life divine.

The Arrow and the Song
Henry Wadsworth Longfellow

I shot an arrow into the air,
It fell to earth, I knew not where;
For, so swiftly it flew, the sight
Could not follow it in its flight.

I breathed a song into the air,
It fell to earth, I knew not where;
For who has sight so keen and strong,
That it can follow the flight of song?

Long, long afterward, in an oak
I found the arrow, still unbroke;
And the song, from beginning to end,
I found again in the heart of a friend.

Be the Best
Douglas Malloch

If you can't be a pine on the top of the hill,
Be a scrub in the valley .. but be
The best little scrub by the side of the rill;
Be a bush if you can't be a tree.

If you can't be a bush, be a bit of the grass,
And some highway happier make;
If you can't be a muskie, then just a bass..
But the liveliest bass in the lake!

We can't all be captains, we've got to be crew,
There's something for all of us here,
There's big work to do, and there's lesser to do
and the task you must do, is the near.

If you can't be a highway, then just be a trail,
If you can't be the sun, be a star;
It isn't by size that you win or your fail...
Be the best of what ever you are!

The Law
Ella Wheeler Wilcox

Your path may be clouded, uncertain your goal;
Move on, for the orbit is fixed for your soul.
And though it may lead into darkness of night,
The torch of the Builder shall give it new light.

You were, and you will be: know this while you are.
Your spirit has traveled both long and afar.
It came from the Source, to the Source it returns;
The spark that was lighted, eternally burns.

From body to body your spirit speeds on;
It seeks a new form where the old one is gone;
And the form that it finds is the fabric you wrought
On the loom of the mind, with the fibre of thought.

You are your own devil, you are your own god,
You fashioned the paths that your footsteps have trod,
And no one can save you from error or sin,
Until you shall hark to the Spirit within.

Somewhere on some planet, sometime and somehow,
Your life will reflect all the thoughts of your now.
The law is unerring; no blood can atone;
The structure you rear, you must live in alone.

from Oud meyer –

" Body to Body our Soul speeds on.
It seeks a new form when the old
          one is gone;
and the form it will find is the fabric
    We've wrought
On the loom of the mind and
      the fibre of thought. "

Our life is like a tapestry of intricate design,
with lovely patterns taking shape
        as colors intertwine.

Some of the threads we weave ourselves
        By things we choose to do.
Sometimes a loving Father's touch
        adds a special hue.

And though tomorrow's pattern
        is not for us to see.
We can trust His perfect hand
        through all eternity.

                    Verse on a sunshine card
                    Author unknown

If you love, you will be loved;
If you respect people, you will be respected;
If you serve them, you will be served;
If you give a good account of yourself toward others,
 Others will act likewise toward you.
Blessed is the man who loves
 and does not desire to be loved for it;
Blessed is he who respects others
 and does not look for respect in return;
Who serves and does not expect service for it;
Who acquits himself well of others
 and does not desire that they return the grace.
Because such things are big,
 foolish people do not rise to them.

Brother Giles

A SMILE

A smile has power ....
 It cost nothing but creates much.
It happens in a flash
 and the memory sometimes lasts forever,
It increases happiness, fosters good will,
 and is the countersign of friends.
It is rest to the weary, daylight to the discouraged,
 sunshine to the sad,
 and a natural antidote for trouble.
Yet it cannot be bought, begged, borrowed or stolen...
 For it is no earthly good to any until given away,
So let's all be generous with our smiles.

Unknown author

Prayer of St Francis

Lord, make me an instrument of thy peace.
Where there is hatred, let me sow love;
where there is injury, pardon;
where there is doubt, faith;
where there is despair, hope;
where there is darkness, light;
where there is sadness, joy.

Oh Divine Master,
grant that I may not so much seek
to be consoled as to console;
to be understood as to understand;
to be loved as to love.
For it is in giving that we receive;
It is in pardoning that we are pardoned;
It is in dying that we are born to eternal life.
Amen

Do all the good you can,
By all the means you can,
In all the ways you can,
In all the places you can,
At all the times you can,
To all the people you can,
As long as ever you can.

John Wesley

He who teaches a child to be thrifty and economical has already bequeathed him a fortune. There is a dignity about saving money. It develops not only a spirit of independence and self-reliance, but it gives you satisfaction to know that you are providing for comfort and security in future years. Every victory over extravagance will give you a distinct moral uplift and raise you in your own estimation.

Grenville Kleiser

No more effort is required to aim high in life,
To demand abundance and prosperity,
Than is required to accept misery and poverty.

Napoleon Hill

I have concluded that the accumulation of wealth, even if I could achieve it, is an insufficient reason for living. When I reach the end of my days, a moment or two from now, I must look backward on some- thing more meaningful that the pursuit of houses and land and machines and stocks and bonds. Nor is fame of any lasting benefit. I will consider my earthly existence to have been wasted unless I can recall a loving family, a consistent investment in the lives of people, and an earnest attempt to serve the God who made me. Nothing else makes much sense.

James Dobson, Jr.

I believe profoundly, that each of us has a mission to perform so long as he live. It is to take the foundation God gives us at birth, and make of it, by discipline such light as we let into our soul, such reason as we cultivate by nurturing our minds with good thoughts and distilled wisdom of others and our own; by consciously lifting ourselves to the spiritual summits achieved by God and His good people.. thus to make and strengthen ourselves so that in our time on this troubled planet we will have given to it something more than just our labor, and our material accomplishments, something that can be measured as good in the sight of our God.

Louis B. Seltzer, Cleveland Press

My Wages
Jessie B. Rittenhouse

I bargained with life for a penny,
and life would pay me no more,
However I begged at evening
when I counted my scanty store.
For life is just an employer,
he gives you what you ask;
But once you have set the wages,
why, you must bear the task.
I worked for a menial's hire,
only to learn, dismayed,
That any wage I had asked of life,
life would have willingly paid.

The Guy in the Glass
Peter Dale Wimbrow Sr.

When you get what you want in your struggle for pelf,
And the world makes you king for a day,

Just go to a mirror and look at yourself
And see what that guy has to say.

For it isn't your father or mother or wife
Whose judgment upon you must pass,

The fellow whose verdict counts most in your life
Is the one staring back from the glass.

Some people might think you're a straight-shootin' chum
And call you a wonderful guy.

But the man in the glass says you're only a bum
If you can't look him straight in the eye.

He's the fellow to please, never mind all the rest
For he's with you clear to the end,

And you've passed your most dangerous test
If the guy in the glass is your friend.

You may fool the whole world down the pathway of years
And get pats on the back as you pass,

But your final reward will be heartache and tears
If you've cheated the guy in the glass.

ATTITUDE
Charles Swindoll

The longer I live, the more I realize the impact of attitude on life. Attitude, to me, is more important than facts. It is more important than the past, than money, than circumstances, than failures, than success, than what other people think or say or do.

It is more important than appearance, giftedness or skill. It will make or break a company, a church, a home, or an individual. The remarkable thing is we have a choice every day regarding the attitude we will embrace for that day.

We cannot change our past ... we cannot change the fact that people will act in a certain way. We cannot change the inevitable. The only thing we can do is play on the one string we have, and that is our attitude.

I am convinced that life is 10% what happens to me and 90% how I react to it. And so it is with you .

We are in charge of our attitudes.

*God grant me the **Serenity**
to accept the things I cannot change,
the **Courage** to change the things I can;
and the **Wisdom** to know the difference.*

Reinhold Neibuhr

The Station

Tucked away in our subconscious minds is an idyllic vision. We see ourselves on a long, long trip that almost spans the continent. We're traveling by passenger train, and out the windows we drink in the passing scene of cars on nearby highways, of children waving at a crossing, of cattle grazing on a distant hillside, of smoke pouring from a power plant, of row upon row of corn and wheat, of flatlands and valleys, of mountains and rolling hills, of biting winter and blazing summer and cavorting spring and docile fall.

But uppermost in our minds is the final destination. On a certain day at a certain hour we will pull into the station. There will be bands playing, and flags waving. And once we get there so many wonderful dreams will come true. So many wishes will be fulfilled and so many pieces of our lives finally will be neatly fitted together like a completed jigsaw puzzle. How restlessly we pace the aisles, damming the minutes for loitering ..waiting, waiting, waiting, for the station.

However, sooner or later we must realize there is no one station, no one place to arrive at once and for all. The true joy of life is the trip. The station is only a dream. It constantly outdistances us.

The Station (continued)

"When we reach the station, that will be it!" we cry.
Translated it means, "When I'm 18, that will be it!'
When I buy a new 450SL Mercedes Benz, that will be it!
When I put the last kin through college that will be it!
When I have paid off the mortgage, that will be it!
When I win a promotion that will be it! When I reach
the age of retirement that will be it! I shall live happily
ever after!

Unfortunately, once we get 'it', then it disappears.
The station somehow hides itself at the end of a endless
track.

"Relish the moment" is a good motto, especially when
coupled with Psalm 118:24: "This is the day which the
Lord hath made; we will rejoice and be glad in it." It
isn't the burdens of today that drive men mad. Rather,
it is regret over yesterday or fear of tomorrow. Regret
and fear are twin thieves who would rob us of today.

So stop pacing the aisles and counting the miles.
Instead, climb more mountains, eat more ice cream, go
barefoot oftener, swim more rivers, watch more
sunsets, laugh more and cry less.   Life must be lived
as we go along. The station will come soon enough.

  Robert J. Hastings
  (Los Angeles Time Syndicate)

Good Posture
Audrey E. Stehle

Clothes don't make a woman
Nor do they make a man.
But do believe this, honey,
Good posture can.

A person who stands tall
Stands out in any crowd;
Companions who are with him
Have reason to be proud.

Good posture instills confidence,
It gives you dignity,
You feel more certain of yourself
And your ability.

Good posture shows to others
What you think of yourself.
So hold your head high, step right out;
Don't be left on the shelf.

Anyone can be in fashion
and be passed without a glance,
But you can't ignore good posture
Nor a figure so enhanced.

Give me a good digestion, Lord,
    and also something to digest;
Give me a healthy body, Lord,
    and sense to keep it, at its best.

Give me a healthy mind, good Lord,
    to keep the good and pure in sight;
Which, seeing sin, is not appalled,
    but finds a way to set it right.

Give me a mind that is not bound,
    that does not whimper, whine or sigh.
Don't let me worry overmuch
    about the fussy thing called I.

Give me a sense of humor, Lord;
    give me the grace to see a joke;
To get some happiness from life
    and pass it on to other folk.

Prayer by Thomas H. B. Webb

A garden for daily living

Plant five rows of peas
        Preparedness
        Promptness
        Perseverance
        Politeness
        Prayer

Plant four rows of squash
        Squash gossip
        Squash indifference
        Squash grumbling
        Squash selfishness

Plant five rows of lettuce
        Lettuce be faithful
        Lettuce be kind
        Lettuce be happy
        Lettuce be truthful
        Lettuce love one another

No garden should be without turnips
        Turnip for service when needed
        Turnip to help one another
        Turnip the music and dance

Water freely with patience and
        cultivate with love
There is much fruit in your garden
Because you reap what you sow

To conclude, in your garden you must have thyme
        Thyme for fun
        Thyme for rest
        Thyme for ourselves

Author unknown

Heaven's Grocery List

I came upon a sign that read Heaven's Grocery store.
When I got a little closer the doors swung open wide,
And when I came to myself I was standing inside.
I saw a host of angels; They were standing everywhere.
One handed me a basket and said, "My child, shop with care."

Everything a human needed was in that grocery store,
And what you could not carry, you could come back for more.

First, I got some **Patience**. **Love** was in that same row.
Further down was **Understanding**,
     you need that everywhere you go.
I got a box or two of **Wisdom** and **Faith** a bag or two.
And **Charity**, of course, I would need some of that, too.

I couldn't miss the **Holy Ghost**; He was all over the place. And
then some **Strength** and **Courage**
     to help me run the race.
My basket was getting full but I remembered I needed **Grace**.
And then I chose **Salvation,** for salvation was for free.
So I tried to get enough of that to do for you and me.

Then I started to the counter to pay my grocery bill,
for I thought I had everything to do the Master's will.
As I went up the aisle I saw **Prayer** and put that in,
for I knew when I stepped outside I would run into sin.

Peace and **Joy** were plentiful, the last things on the shelf.
Song and **Praise** were hanging near so I just helped my-
self.

Then I said to the angel "Now how much do I owe?"
He smiled and said, "Just take them everywhere you go."
Again I asked, "Really now, how much do I owe?"
"My child," he said, "God paid your bill, a long, long time ago."

Author unknown

Count your blessings, instead of your crosses
Count your gains, instead of you losses
Count your joys, instead of your woes
Count your friends, instead of your foes
Count your smiles, instead of your tears
Count your full years, instead of the lean
Count your kind deeds, instead of the mean
Count your health, instead of your wealth
Count on God, instead of yourself.

Author unknown

To live well we must have a faith fit to live by, a self fit to live with, and a work fit to live for, something to which we can give ourselves and thus get ourselves off our hands.

We cannot tell what may happen to us in the strange medley of life, but we can decide what happens in us, how we can take it, what we do with it, and that is what really counts in the end. How to take the raw stuff of life and make it a thing of worth and beauty. That is the test of living. Life is an adventure of faith, if we are to be victors over it, not victims of it. Faith in the God above us, faith in the little infinite soul within us, faith in life and in our fellow souls... without faith, the plus quality, we cannot live.

John Fort Newton

Optimism
Ella Wheeler Wilcox

Talk happiness. The world is sad enough without your woes. No path is wholly rough; look for the places that are smooth and clear, and speak of those, to rest the weary ear of earth, so hurt by one continuous strain of human discontent and grief and pain.

Talk faith. The world is better off without your uttered ignorance and morbid doubt. If you have faith in God, or man, or self, say so. If not, push back upon the shelf of silence all you thoughts, 'til faith shall come; no one will ever grieve because your lips are dumb.

Talk health. The dreary, never-changing tale of mortal maladies is worn and stale. You cannot charm, or interest, or please by harping on that minor chord, disease. Say you are well, or all is well with you, and God shall hear your words and make them true.

I am only one, but still I am one.
I cannot do everything,
but still I can do something;
And because I cannot do everything,
I will not refuse to do the something that I can do.

Edward Everett Hale

Five Steps to Wisdom

"Hear, read, mark, learn and inwardly digest"

People in the foreign service have to do a great deal of listening. TO HEAR is often more profitable than to talk. Even when it is not, there is advantage if the other man feels that he has not only been listened to, but has been heard. If the decision goes against him, he has at least presented his case, and his disappointment will not be tinged with resentment.

TO READ AND TO MARK: these words are so familiar that it is easy to forget their inwardness. How often does a summary or a secondhand remark, distort the meaning of a speech, a statement or an official paper. No man can now a days read everything he should. But a careful perusal of selected original work is more rewarding than a summary of wider range. It encourages the marking, whether on the paper or in the mind's eye; of those significant points, those finer shades of meaning, which the cursory reader can so easily overlook.

That which we LEARN from what we have read and marked will, of course, depend as much upon our gift of selection. Yet if we have first learned to distinguish a precise commitment for an expression of pious hope; an official statement from an individual opinion; publicity from propaganda; an editorial from a news story; an eye witness account from one written a thousand miles away; then we shall at least have a better chance of getting to the heart of the matter.

But the most important function of all is that of INWARD DIGESTION. That chewing of the cud, which converts, by the process of reflection, what one has read, marked, and learned, into judgment or action. Digestion is, with most of us, a slow business. There are those of us who can absorb quickly, come to a decision quickly and then act quickly. We all have to do so now and then. But it is only by mental digestion, within one's own system, that the raw material of things learned, the semi-processed material of things reflected upon, can be transformed into that occasional gem, an addition to our small stock of wisdom.

By Sir Roger Makins (British Ambassador to U. S.)

☆☆☆☆☆☆☆☆☆☆☆
☆   ☆

Most Important Sentences

1. What is your opinion?
2. How can I help?
3. You are special !
4. Thank you

Least Important Sentences

1. "I ......"

☆☆☆☆☆☆☆☆☆☆☆

Remember your ABCs
Wanda Carter

Avoid negative sources, people, places, things and habits.
Believe in yourself.
Consider things from every angle
Don't give up, and don't give in.
Enjoy life today, yesterday is gone,
      and tomorrow may never come.
Family and friends are hidden treasures.
      Seek them and enjoy their riches.
Give more than you plan to give.
Hang on to your dreams.
Ignore those who try to discourage you.
Just do it.
Keep on trying, no matter how hard it seems,
      it all will get easier.
Love yourself first and most.
Make it happen.
Never lie, cheat, or steal. Always strike a fair deal.
Open your eyes and see things as they really are.
Practice makes perfect.
Quitters never win, and winners never quit.
Read, study and learn about everything important
      in your life.
Stop procrastinating.
Take control of your own destiny.
Understand yourself in order to better understand others.
Visualize it.
Want it more than anything.
Xcellerate your efforts.
You are unique of all of God's creation.
      Nothing can replace you.
Zero in on your target, and go for it.

The Girl Scout Promise

On my honor, I will try:
To do my duty to God and my country,
To help other people at all times,
To obey the Girl Scout Laws.

The Girl Scout Laws

1. A Girl Scout's honor is to be trusted.
2. A Girl Scout is loyal.
3. A Girl Scout's duty is to be useful and to help others.
4. A Girl Scout is a friend to all and a sister to every other Girl Scout.
5. A Girl Scout is courteous.
6. A Girl Scout is a friend to animals.
7. A Girl Scout obeys orders.
8. A Girl Scout is cheerful.
9. A Girl Scout is thrifty.
10. A Girl Scout is clean in thought, word, and deed.

O Lord,

Grant that each one who has to do with me today may be the happier for it.

Let it be given me each hour today what I shall say, and grant me the wisdom of a loving heart that I may say the right thing rightly.

Help me to enter into the mind of everyone who talks with me, and keep me alive to the feelings of each one present.

Give me a quick eye for the little kindness that I may be ready in doing them and gracious in receiving them.

Give me a quick perception of feelings and needs of others, and make me eager hearted in helping them.

Amen

Author unknown

Hearts like doors open with ease...
With "I thank you" and
    "If you please"

DESIDERATA
Max Ehrmann

Go placidly amid the noise and haste, and remember what peace there may be in silence. As far as possible, without surrender, be on good terms with all persons. Speak your truth quietly and clearly; and listen to others, even to the dull and ignorant; they too have their story.

Avoid loud and aggressive persons, they are vexations to the spirit. If you compare yourself with others, you may become vain and bitter, for always there will be greater and lesser persons than yourself. Enjoy your achievements as well as your plans.

Keep interested in your own career, however humble; it is a real possession in the changing fortunes of time. Exercise caution in your business affairs, for the world is full of trickery. But let this not blind you to what virtue there is; many persons strive for high ideals, and everywhere life is full of heroism.

Be yourself. Especially do not feign affection. Neither be cyn-ical about love; for in the face of all aridity and disenchantment it is a perennial as the grass. Take kindly the counsel of the years, gracefully surrendering the things of youth. Nurture strength of spirit to shield you in sudden misfortune. But do not distress yourself with dark imaginings. Many fears are born of fatigue and loneliness.

Beyond a wholesome discipline, be gently with yourself. You are a child of the universe no less than the trees and the stars; you have a right to be here. And whether or not it is clear to you, no doubt the universe is unfolding as it should.

Therefore be at peace with God, whatever you conceive Him to be. And whatever your labors and aspirations, in the noisy confusion of life, keep peace with your soul. With all its sham, drudgery and broken dreams, it is still a beautiful world. Be cheerful. Strive to be happy.

The Man Who Thinks He Can
Walter Wintle

If you think you are beaten, you are
If you think you dare not, you don't
If you'd like to win, but think you can't
It's almost a cinch you won't
Life little battles don't always go
To the stronger or faster man
But sooner or later, the man who wins
Is the man who thinks he can.

ᏝᏝᏝᏝ

You Mustn't Quit

When things go wrong, as they sometimes will,
When the road you're trudging seems all uphill,
When funds are low and the debts are high,
And you want to smile but you have to sigh,
When troubles are pressing you down a bit ..
Rest if you must, but do not quit.

Success is failure turned inside out,
The silver tint of the clouds of doubt
You can never tell how close you are,
It may be near when it seems afar
So stay in the fight when you're hardest hit
It's when things seem worst that you mustn't quit.

Author unknown

It Couldn't Be Done
Edgar A. Guest

Somebody said that it couldn't be done
But he with a chuckle replied
That "maybe it couldn't" but he would be one
Who wouldn't say so till he'd tried.

So he buckled right in with the trace of a grin
On his face. If he worried, he hid it
He started to sing as he tackled the thing
That couldn't be done, and he did it.

Somebody scoffed: "Oh, you'll never do that,
At least no one ever has done it";
But he took off his coat and he took off his hat
And the first thing we knew he'd begun it.

With a lift of his chin and a bit of a grin
Without any doubting or quiddit
He started to sing as he tackled the thing
That couldn't be done, and he did it.

There are thousands to tell you it cannot be done
There are thousands to prophesy failure
There are thousands to point out to you one by one
The dangers that wait to assail you.

But just buckle in with a bit of a grin
Just take off your coat and go to it
Just start in to sing as you tackle the thing
That "cannot be done" and you'll do it.

The New Year
Nick Kenny

I am the New Year
A blank sheet of paper
On which to write the great American novel
Or paint an immortal masterpiece
Or just let me remain blank

I am a newly minted coin
To be spent foolishly in a day
Or invested in happy plans for a lifetime

I am twelve shining months
Which can be your stairway to the stars
Or a dead-end street to oblivion

I am the New Year
Three hundred and sixty five days
In which to make a dream come true

A fresh start..
So, make the best of me
Hold on tightly to your heart
Or let me slip through your careless fingers
Like the sands of time

I am the New Year

The day will bring some lovely thing,
I say it over, each new dawn
Some gay adventurous thing
to hold against my heart when it is gone.

And so I rise and go to meet
The day with wings upon my feet.
I come upon it unaware ..
Some sudden beauty without name;
A snatch of song, a breath of pine;
A poem lit with golden flame;
High tangled bird notes, keenly timed..

Like flying color on the wing.
No day has ever failed me quite..

Before the grayest day is done,
I come upon some misty bloom
Or a late streak of crimson sun
Each night I pause, remembering
Some gay, adventurous, lovely thing!
No day has failed me yet.

Grace Noll Crowell
(from Marjorie Herman)

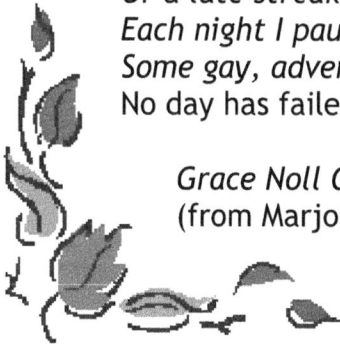

I still find each day too short for all the thoughts
I want to think, for all the walks I want to take,
for all the books I want to read, and all the
friends I want to see.

John Burroughs

If you have a tender message or a loving word to say,
Don't wait 'till you forget it, but whisper it today.
Tomorrow is a mystery, today is all we own,
We are living in the present, the future is unknown,
The tender word unspoken, the letter never sent.
The long forgotten messages,
      the wealth of love unspent,
For these some heart is breaking,
      for these some loved ones wait,
So show them that you care today, before it is too late.

Author unknown

Be swift, dear heart in loving, for time is brief,
And thou mayst soon along life's highway
     keep step with grief.

Be swift, dear heart in saying the kindly word.
When ears are sealed, your passionate pleasing
     will not be heard.

Be swift, dear heart in doing the gracious deed.
Lest soon they whom thou holdest dearest
     be past the need.

Dear heart, be swift in loving; time speedest on,
And all thy chance of blessed service will be gone.

Author unknown

Bring me all your Flowers now
R. D. Richards

I would rather have a single rose
From a flower garden of a friend
Than have the choicest flowers
When my stay on earth must end.

I would rather have the kindest words
Which may now be said to me,
Than flattered when my heart is still
And, this life has ceased to be.

I would rather have a loving smile
From the friends I know are true
Than tears shed 'round my casket,
When this world I've bade adieu.

Bring me all your flowers,
Whether pink or white or red
I'd rather have one blossom now
Than a truckload when I'm dead!

*I expect to pass through this world but once,
any good therefore that I can do, or any
kindness that I show to any fellow creature,
let me do it now. Let me not defer or neglect
it, for I shall not pass this way again.*

William Penn

If you're ever going to love me love me now, while I can know all the sweet and tender feelings which from real affection flow.

Love me now, while I am living; do not wait till I am gone and then chisel in the marble.. warm love words on ice-cold stone.

If you've dear, sweet thoughts about me, why not whisper them to me? Don't you know 'twould make me happy and as glad as glad can be?

If you wait till I am sleeping, ne'er to waken here again, There'll be walls of earth between us and I couldn't hear you then.

If you knew some one was thirsting for a drop of water sweet, would you be so slow to bring it? Would you step with laggard feet?

There are tender hearts all around us who are thirsting for our love; Why withhold from them what nature makes them crave all else above?

I won't need your kind caresses when the grass grows o'er my face; I won't crave your love or kisses in my last low resting place.

So, then, if you love me any, if it's but a little bit, let me know it while I'm living, I can own and treasure it.

Author unknown

The Land of Beginning Again
Louisa Fletcher

I wish that there were some wonderful place
Called the Land of Beginning Again,
Where all our mistakes and all our heartaches
And all our poor selfish grief,
Could be dropped like a shabby old coat by the door,
And never be put on again.

I wish that we could come on it all unaware,
Like the hunter who finds a lost trail;
And I wish that the one whom our blindness had done
The greatest injustice of all could be at the gates,
Like an old friend that waits
For the comrade he's gladdest to hail.

We would find all the things we intended to do,
But forgot, and remembered too late;
Little praises unspoken and promises broken,
All of the thousand and one
Small duties neglected that might have perfected
The day for one less fortunate.

It wouldn't be possible not to be kind
In the Land of Beginning Again; And the ones we misjudged,
And the ones whom we grudged their moments of victory here,
Would find in the grasp of our loving hand-clasp
More than penitent lips could explain.

For what had been hardest we'd know had been best
And what once had seemed lost was but gain
For there isn't a sting that will not take wing
When we've faced it and laughed it away
And I think, too, that laughter is most what we're after,
In the Land of Beginning Again.

So I wish that there were some wonderful place
Called the Land of Beginning Again,
Where all our mistakes and all our heartaches
And all of our poor selfish grief,
Could be dropped like a shabby old coat at the door
And never be put on again!

From Harold's mother's scrapbook

God's Design
Helen Steiner Rice

Into our lives come many things, to break the dull routine,
The things we had not planned on, that happen unforeseen.

The unexpected little joys that are scattered on our way,
Success we did not count on .... or a rare, fulfilling day.

A catchy, lilting melody that makes us want to dance,
A nameless exaltation of enchantment and romance.

An unsought word of kindness, a complement or two
That sets the eyes to gleaming like crystal drops of dew....

The unplanned sudden meeting that comes with sweet surprise,
And lights the heart with happiness like a rainbow in the skies.

Now some folks call it fickle fate and some folks call it chance,
While others just accept it, as pleasant happenstance .....

But no matter what you call it, it didn't come without design,
For all our lives are fashioned by the Hand that is divine;

And every happy happening and every lucky break
Are little gifts from God above that are ours to freely take.

Did you think it would be forgotten?
That no mention would be made?
No one yelling "Surprise Party"
Or jumping out of a cake?

For balloons and decorations
You'd be waiting the whole day long ..
Not thinking you'd get a special wish
With this Happy Birthday song
When you blow out the candles,
May your special wish come true,
It's your day to be the star,
A "Happy Birthday to you"

Author unknown

Count your garden by the flowers,
    never by the leaves that fall.
Count your days by golden hours,
    don't remember clouds at all!
Count your nights by stars, not shadows;
    count your life with smiles, not tears;
And with joy on this, your birthday,
    count your age by friends, not years.

Author unknown

Happy Birthday!

It certainly is a happy day. The celebration of the day of your birth. On that day, at that time, God placed on this great planet earth a very special creature.... you!

He breathed the breath of His life into your being, and in so doing bestowed upon you the gift of Himself. The divine nature of God has been recreated in you by Him!

Is this not something to celebrate? This is your day to remember God's gift to you at your birth .. the gift of His own divine nature.

Why are you looking for happiness? You have happiness. You have given it to others. How can you give something unless you have it to give?

Why are you looking for love? You have love, you are love. This, too, you have given to others and again... to give it, you must have it. Do you see how complete and how wonderful you really are?

As you celebrate *this wonderful you* that you are, remember, the source of this very special you is God! As you start showing forth this Spirit of God, that is within you, it will start working in your life to produce great things.

Always remember to acknowledge that the power working for you is God's power, not yours. If you should claim power and glory it produces as yours, the flow will stop.

While you are acknowledging Him in all your ways, you are putting your life in His hands and letting Him guide and direct you, and all will be well.

This will happen only when you get yourself out of the way and let Him flow through you as you. Yes, as you, God is within all of us, but we all express Him in our own individual way.

Happy Birthday! (continued)

There is not another human being in the world who is exactly like you, so there is not another human being in the world who will express God within exactly as you do.

You may share characteristics with a number of people, but not all their characteristics. You are different. You are unique. You are special. God has ordained it so, and so it is.

All persons can give happiness to others, but not in exactly the same way that you can. Other people can give love, but never in just your way. Everyone's way of expressing the Spirit of God within them is needed. Your individual way is needed. This is the Christ within you .... your individual expression of the Spirit of God that dwells within you.

Congratulations on being you! The world had need of you, for you are a part of the whole and the world is not complete without you. When you know this, doesn't it give you a different attitude about the world and everybody and everything in it?

The world is waiting to receive your divine nature, the Christ in you.

Author unknown

If You Stand Very Still
Patience Strong

If you stand very still in the heart of the woods,
  you will hear many wonderful things ..
The snap of a twig and the wind in the trees
  and whir of invisible wings.

If you stand very still in the turmoil of life
  and wait for the voice from within,
You will be led down the pathways of wisdom and peace
  in a mad world of chaos and din.

If you stand very still and hold to your faith,
  you will get all the help that you ask.
You will draw from the silence the things that you need...
  hope and courage and strength for your task.

The Butterfly

Of all the ways that things may grow and change
I think the butterfly grows in much the strangest way
First it's just a crawly bug
That crawls into a little brown hole
But when it comes to light again
It's wondrous to see
It has changed into a butterfly
It is very strange to me.

Author unknown

Childhood leaves many deep impressions. I am grateful to my ~~father~~ parents for ~~his~~ their deep religious impact on our family.

One occasion I recall was a gentle awakening in the night, warmly blanketed, to see the magnificent sky in all its splendor. Always such an experience was related to God's place in our lives. We were taught to believe that our lives should radiate a gleam - - just as the stars - - and that a good life was the only kind that could reflect God's goodness.

As we grew older the glorious phenomena of nature took on a living personality. Very early our guided thoughts were given a deeper meaning........out in the vast space was GOD, He stood by us when needed and somehow He was in us to strengthen and reassure. My parents +

My father had made religion a real and meaningful experience. As a parent I have passed this experience on to our childre, who have benefited.

Prayer: "O Lord, Grant that each one who has to do with me today may be happier for it. Grant me the wisdom of a loving heart. Give me a quick eye for little kindnesses that I may be ready in doing and gracious in receiving. Give me a quick perception of the feelings and needs of others, and make me eager-hearted in helping them. Amen."

O Jina Kirkstadt

Kingsley Couples Lenten Booklet
Church of the Saviour
Cleveland Heights, Ohio
January 1962

ENJOY NATURE   PAGE 65

The Daffodils
William Wordsworth

I wandered lonely as a cloud
That floats on high o're vales and hills,
When all at once I saw a crowd,
A host, of golden daffodils;
Beside the lake, beneath the trees,
Fluttering and dancing in the breeze.

Continuous as the stars that shine
And twinkle on the milky way,
They stretched in never-ending line
Along the margin of a bay:
Ten thousand saw I at a glance,
Tossing their heads in sprightly dance.

The waves beside them danced; but they
Outdid the sparkling waves in glee:
A poet could not but be gay,
In such a jocund company:
I gazed – and gazed – but little thought
What wealth the show to me had brought:

For oft, when on my couch I lie
In vacant or in pensive mood,
They flash upon that inward eye
Which is the bliss of solitude:
And then my heart with pleasure fills,
And dances with the daffodils.

ENJOY NATURE

Four Leaf Clovers

I know a place where the sun is like gold
And the cherry blooms burst forth with snow;
And down underneath is the loveliest nook,
Where the four-leafed clovers grow.

One leaf is for **Hope**, and one is for **Faith**
And one is for **Love**, you know,
And God put another one in for **Luck**,
If you search you'll find where they grow.

But you must have hope, and you must have faith,
You must love and be strong, and so
If you work, if you wait, you'll find the place,
Where the four-leaf clovers grow.

Ella Higginson

Note from Carol...
Mother frequently looked for 4 leaf clovers and found them.
She had a collection of about 20 clovers pressed in a small
notebook.

The Creation
Cecil Frances Alexander

All things bright and beautiful,
All creatures, great and small,
All things wise and wonderful,
The Lord God made them all.

Each little flower that opens
Each little bird that sings
He made their glowing colors
He made their tiny wings.

The rich man in his castle
The poor man at his gate,
God made them, high or lowly,
And ordered their estate.

The purple-headed mountain,
The river running by
The sunset and the morning
That brightens up the sky.

The cold wind in the winter
The pleasant summer sun
The ripe fruits in the garden
He made them every one.

The tall trees in the greenwood
The meadows where we play
The rushes by the water
We gather every day.

He gave us eyes to see them
And lips that we might tell
How great is God Almighty
Who has made all things well!

Trees

I think that I shall never see
A poem lovely as a tree.

A tree whose hungry mouth is prest
Against the earth's sweet flowing breast;

A tree that looks at God all day,
And lifts her leafy arms to pray;

A tree that may in summer wear
A nest of robins in her hair;

Upon whose bosom snow has lain;
Who intimately lives with rain.

Poems are made by fools like me,
But only God can make a tree.

Joyce Kilmer

THANK YOU, DEAR
Kay Lipke Warren

"Thank you, Dear", these words are the most important of all in any really happy marriage. In the tense and worrisome world in which we live. I often wonder if we have not forgotten how to love, how to enjoy deeply the little happiness which come along from day to day in a marriage and may go unnoticed and unappreciated.

We plan feverishly for the future, saving our money for the larger house, the new car, for new clothes, or the latest shining equipment in the kitchen, forgetting that marriage itself sometimes needs a renewal, a bit of nourishment, too. And that comes, not so much from the exchange of things as of feelings and thoughts...warm, affectionate, grateful.

It is a rewarding experience to remember, and to say "Thank you", for the human side of married life. Here for example are some of the thankful things I like to say to my husband .. sometimes silently, sometimes out loud. I've found they can add greatly to the richness and joy of married life:

1. *Thank you* for living with me all year.
2. *Thank you* for your loyalty and patience,
     even when I may be irritable and unreasonable.
3. *Thank you* for not demanding more of me
     than I can give
4. *Thank you* for minimizing my faults
     and magnifying my virtues
5. *Thank you* for looking after me sympathetically
     when I am ill.
6. *Thank you* for not slapping me down unkindly
     when my ego is showing.
7. *Thank you* for being proud of me
     and of our marriage after all these years
8. *Thank you* for everything
9. *Thank you*, dear, for you.

The Marriage Creed
Emanuel & Virginia L. Feldman (1971)

♥ *Comfort each other* Provide a refuge and sanctuary for each
other from the chill winds of the world. Your marriage is a
hearth, from whence comes the peace, harmony, and warmth
of soul and spirit.

♥ *Caress as you would be caressed* Warm your loved one's
body with your healing touch. Remember that as babies can
die with lack of touching, so can marriages wither from lack of
closeness.

♥ *Be a friend and partner* Friendship can be a peaceful island,
separate and apart, in a world of turmoil and strife. Reflect
upon the tranquility of the many future years you can share
with a true friend, and beware of becoming battling enemies
under the same roof.

♥ *Be open with each other* Bind not yourselves in the
secretness that causes suspicion and doubt. Trust and reveal
yourselves to each other, even as the budding rose opens to
reveal it's fragrance and beauty.

♥ *Listen to each other* Hear not only words, but also the non-
language of tone, mood, and expression. Learn to listen to
understand rather than listening to argue.

♥ *Respect each other's rights* Remember that each is a person
of flesh and blood, entitled to his or her own choices and
mistakes. Each owns himself, and has the right to equality.

♥ *Allow the other to be an individual* Seek not to create for
each other a new mold that can only fit with much discomfort
and pain. Accept the other as they are, as you would have
yourself accepted.

♥ *Give each other approval* Remember criticism divides,
while compliments encourage confidence in the other. Hasten
not to point out the other mistakes, for each will soon discover
his own.

♥ *Cherish your union* Let no one come between your
togetherness. Not child, not friend nor worldly goods. Yet
maintain enough separateness to allow each other his or her
own unique oneness.

♥ *Love one another* Love is your river of life, your eternal
source of recreation yourselves. Above all else love one
another.

BLESS THIS HOUSE

In care and pleasure, great and small;
Blest be the door friends enter by
And the windows that let in the sky;
And roof above and walls about
That shut the world and weather out!

Lord, make my house a mansion
Of abiding loveliness and love,
A friendly, comfortable place.
Let pleasant talk like firelight grace
These rooms, and may friends linger long
To join in laughter or a song.

Blest be these rooms for work or play!
Oh, let my house be sometimes gay,
And sometimes still as candlelight.
Be with us, Lord, both day and night.

Blest be our labor and our rest
Our waking and our sleep be blest
In care and pleasure, great and small
Lord, bless this house and bless us all!

Author unknown

If there is righteousness in the
heart, there will be beauty in the
character. If there be beauty in the
character, there will be harmony in
the family home. If there is harmony
in the home, there will be order in
the nation. When there is order in
the nation, there will be peace in the
world.

Ancient proverb (Confucius)

"It is not so much about the house,
    That anyone can see;
Its' not so much about the ground
    That calls the birds & bees.
Its' just the folks that live within
    and flower that blooms without
That calls the bird, and best friends,
    Thats what we care about."
                        Carrie Jacobs Bond —

And since I have no gold to give
And love alone must make amends,
My only prayer is while I live,
God make me worthy of my friends.

Author unknown

They talk about a woman's sphere
As though it had a limit
There's not a place on earth or heaven
There's not a task to mankind given
There's not a blessing or a woe
There's not a whispered yes or no
There's not a life or death or birth
That has a feather's weight of worth
Without a woman in it

Kate Field

Hello, Mrs. Jones, I've just called to say
I'm sorry I cried when you phoned today

No, I didn't get angry when your call came at four,
Just as eight cub scouts burst through the door

It's just that I had such a really full day
I'd baked eight pies for the P. T. A.

And washing and ironing and scrubbing the floor
Were chores I had finished not too long before

The reason I cried and gave out a big yelp…
Was not cause you phoned just to ask for my help

The comment that just about drove me berserk
Was **"I'm sure you'll have time because you don't work"**

 A happy homemaker

Busy mother poem

I know a busy mother with a thousand daily cares. Who will say each time I meet her, "I've just found some new grey hairs."

It's the housework and the children that are turning my hair gray. All of these problems and this pressure are just wearing me away.

I wonder as I listen while she frets about her curls, if she has ever looked at diamonds, or admired the glow of pearls.

If an oyster has a problem when some sand gets in it's shell, then it covers it with beauty and makes a pearl as well.

And a worthless lump of carbon, hidden deep beneath the earth changes form because of pressure, and a diamond is given birth.

Without problems, without pressures, they'd both have been sand and coal. Let us be thankful that our problems help make a lovely soul.

That Wonderful Mother of Mine
Clyde Hager

You are a wonderful mother,
Dear old Mother of mine.
You'll hold a spot down deep in my heart,
'Til the stars no longer shine.

Your soul shall live on forever,
On through the fields of time.
For there'll never be another to me,
Like that wonderful Mother of mine.

HUGS
Jill Wolf

There's something in a simple hug
That always warms the heart;
It welcomes us back home
And makes it easier to part.

A hug's a way to share the joy
And sad times we go through,
Or just a way for friends to say
They like you 'cause you're you.

Hugs are meant for anyone
For whom we really care,
From your grandma to your neighbor,
Or a cuddly teddy bear.

A hug is an amazing thing,
It's just the perfect way
To show the love we're feeling
But can't find the words to say.

It's funny how a little hug
Makes everyone feel good;
In every place and language,
It's always understood.

And hugs don't need new equipment,
Special batteries or parts,
Just open up your arms
And open up your hearts.

Send them to Bed with a Kiss

O mothers, so weary, discouraged,
Worn out with the cares of the day,
You often grow cross and impatient
Complain of the noise and the play
For the day brings so many vexations
So many things going amiss
But mothers, whatever may vex you
Send the children to bed with a kiss!

The dear little feet wander often
Perhaps from the pathway of right
The dear little hands find new mischief
To try you from morning 'til night
But think of the desolate mothers
Who'd give all the world for your bliss
And, as thanks for your infinite blessings
Send the children to bed with a kiss.

For some day their noise will not vex you
The silence will hurt far more
You will long for their sweet childish voices
For the sweet childish face at the door
And to press a child's face to your bosom
You'd give all the world for just this!
For the comfort 'twill bring you in sorrow,
Send the children to bed with a kiss!

Author unknown

The Builder

A builder builded a temple
He wrought it with grace and skill;
Pillars and groins and arches
All fashioned to work his will
Men said, as they saw its beauty,
'It shall never know decay.
Great is thy skill, O Builder!
Thy fame shall endure for aye.

A teacher builded a temple
With loving and infinite care,
Planning each arch with patience,
Laying each stone with prayer
None praised her unceasing efforts
None know of her wondrous plan
For the temple the teacher builded
Was unseen by the eyes of man.

Gone is the builder's temple,
Crumbled into the dust
Low lies each stately pillar,
Food for consuming rust
But the temple the teacher builded
Will last while the ages roll
For that beautiful unseen temple
Was a child's immortal soul.

Author unknown

If a child lives with criticism, he learns to condemn
If a child lives with hostility, he learns to fight
If a child lives with ridicule, he learns to be shy
If a child lives with shame, he learns to feel guilty
If a child lives with tolerance, he learns to be patient
If a child lives with encouragement, he learns confidence
If a child lives with praise, he learns to appreciate
If a child lives with fairness, he learns justice
If a child lives with security, he learns to have faith
If a child lives with approval, he learns to like himself
If a child lives with acceptance and friendship,
        he learns to find love in the world.

Dorothy Law Nolte

If we work upon marble it will perish.
If we work on brass, time will efface it.
If we raise temples, they will crumble to dust.

But if we work upon man's
        or youth's immortal minds,
If we imbue them with high ideals
        and principles
We engrave on those tablets (minds)
Something which time cannot efface and
        which will brighten to all eternity.

Daniel Webster

"Their wedding was a great affair. The guests came dressed in their best bibs and feathers and stayed way past crowing time."

From "**Little Nog**" by Imogene Wolcott
drawings by Walter Early

The Golden Girl

She's watching all that you say and do
Weighing, surveying the world and you
And absorbing more that you might surmise
The golden girl with the searching eyes.

The cocoon of childhood protects her still
With dreams to which she retreats at will
But has she a treasure to take their place
When tomorrow's world is hers to face?

Give her the gift with the lift of wings
Teach her the love of beautiful things!

Author unknown
(From Ileen Willis February 1966)

I had a Mother who read to me the things
That wholesome life to the boy heart brings.
Stories that stir with an upward touch,
Oh, that each mother of boys were such!

You may have tangible wealth untold;
Caskets of jewels and coffers of gold.
Richer than I you can never be.
I had a Mother who read to me.

Strickland Gillilan

HIAWATHA'S CHILDHOOD
Henry Wadsworth Longfellow

By the shores of Gitchee Gumee,
By the shining Big-Sea-Water,
Stood the wigwam of Nokomis
Daughter of the Moon, Nokomis.
Dark behind it rose the forest,
Rose the black and gloomy pine trees,
Rose the firs with cones upon them;
Bright before it beat the water,
Beat the clear and sunny water,
Beat the shining Big-Sea-Water.

From **A Tree for Peter**
Kate Seredy

"A spade. A little toy spade with a red handle from the five-and-ten-cent store," said Peter Marsh quietly. "It is a story. A long one. About a lame boy, a little red spade, a tiny Christmas tree, and a ... a man nobody knew. Want to hear it?"

From **The Cat that Walked by Himself**
(Just So Stories)

Rudyard Kipling

Hear and attend and listen; for this befell and behappened and became and was, O my Best Beloved, when the Tame animals were wild. The Dog was wild, and the Horse was wild, and the Cow was wild, and the Sheep was wild, and the Pig was wild — as wild as wild could be — and they walked in the Wet Wild Woods by their wild lones. But the wildest of all the wild animals was the Cat. He walked by himself, and all places were alike to him.

Suppose
Phoebe Cary

Suppose, my little lady, your doll should break her head,
Could you make it whole by crying
      'till your eyes and nose were red?
And wouldn't it be pleasanter to treat it as a joke;
And say you're glad 'Twas Dolly's
      and not your head, that broke?"

Suppose you're dressed for walking,
      and the rain comes pouring down,
Will it clear off any sooner because you scold and frown?
And wouldn't it be nicer for you to smile than to pout,
And so make sunshine in the house
      when there is none without?

Suppose your task, my little man, is very hard to get,
Will it make it any easier for you to sit and fret?
And wouldn't it be wiser than waiting like a dunce,
To go to work in earnest and learn a thing at once?

Suppose that some boys have a horse,
      and some a coach and pair,
Will it tire you less while walking to say, "It isn't fair"?
And wouldn't it be nobler to keep your temper sweet,
And in your heart be thankful
      you can walk upon your feet?

And suppose the world don't please you,
      nor the way some people do,
Do you think the whole creation
      will be altered just for you?
And isn't it, my boy or girl, the wisest, bravest plan,
Whatever comes or doesn't come,
      to do the best you can?

Listen to the MUSTN'TS, child,
Listen to the DON'TS
Listen to the SHOULDN'TS
The IMPOSSIBLES, The WON'TS
Listen to the NEVER HAVES
Then listen close to me ..
Anything can happen, child,
ANYTHING can be.

Shel Silverstein (Where the Sidewalk Ends)

The Lost Doll
Charles Kingsley

I once had a sweet little doll, dears,
The prettiest doll in the world.
Her cheeks were so red and so white, dears
And her hair was so charmingly curled.
But I lost my poor little doll, dears
As I played on the heath one day;
And I cried for her more that a week, dears
But I never could find where she lay.

I found my poor little doll, dears
As I played on the heath one day.
Folks say she is terribly changed, dears
For her paint is all washed away.
And her arm trodden off by the cows, dears
And her hair not the least bit curled.
Yet for old time's sake, she is still, dears,
The prettiest doll in the world.

PURPLE COW
Gelett Burgess

I never saw a purple cow,
I never hope to see one
But I can tell you, anyhow,
I'd rather see than be one!

GRASSHOPPER GREEN
Nancy Dingman Watson

Grasshopper Green is a comical chap;
    He lives on the best of fare
Bright little trousers, jacket, and cap,
    These are his summer wear.
Out in the meadow he loves to go
    Playing away in the sun
It's hopperty, skipperty, high and low,
    Summer's the time for fun.

Grasshopper Green has a quaint little house
    It's under the hedge so gay
Grandmother Spider, as still as a mouse,
    Watches him over the way.
Gladly he's calling the children, I know,
    Out in the beautiful sun'
It's hopperty, skipperty, high and low,
    Summer's the time for fun.

ELETELEPHONY
Laura E. Richards

Once there was an elephant,
Who tried to use the telephant ..
No! no! I mean an elephone
Who tried to use the telephone ..
(Dear me! I am not certain quite
That even now I've got it right.)

Howe'er it was, he got his trunk
Entangled in the telephunk;
The more he tried to get it free,
The louder buzzed the telephee ..
(I fear I'd better drop the song
Of elephop and telephong!)

A wise old owl lived in an oak;
The more he saw the less he spoke;
The less he spoke the more he heard;
Why can't we all be like that bird?

Edward Hershey Richards

Mother may I go out to swim?
Yes, my darling daughter
But hang your clothes on a hickory limb
And don't go near the water.

Author unknown

My Shadow

Robert Louis Stevenson

I have a little shadow
that goes in and out with me,
And what can be the use of him
is more than I can see.
He is very, very like me
from the heels up to the head
And I see him jump before me,
when I jump into my bed.

The funniest thing about him
is the way he likes to grow....
Not at all like proper children,
which is always very slow;
For he sometimes shoots up taller
like a India-rubber ball,
And he sometimes gets so little
that there's none of him at all.

He hasn't got a notion
of how children ought to play
And can only make a fool of me
in every sort of way.
He stays so close beside me,
he's a coward you can see
I'd think shame to stick to nursie
as that shadow sticks to me!

One morning, very early,
before the sun was up,
I rose and found the shining dew
on every buttercup.
But my lazy little shadow
Like an arrant sleepyhead
Had stayed at home behind me
and was fast asleep in bed.

THREE LITTLE BUGS
Alice Cary

Three little bugs in a basket
And hardly room for two
And one was yellow, and one was black,
And one like me, or you;
The space was small, no doubt, for all;
So what should the three bugs do?

Three little bugs in a basket,
And the beds but two could hold;
And so they fell to quarreling..
The white, and the black, and the gold
And two of the bugs got under the rugs,
And one was out in the cold!

Three little bugs in a basket,
And hardly crumbs for two
And all were selfish in their hearts
The same as I or you
So the strong ones said, "We'll eat the bread,
And that's what we will do,"

He that was left in the basket,
Without a crumb to chew
Or a thread to wrap himself withal
When the wind across him blew
Pulled one of the rugs from one of the bugs
And so the quarrel grew.

So there was war in the basket
Ah! Pity 'tis 'tis true!
But he that was frozen and starved, at last
A strength from his weakness drew,
And pulled the rugs from both the bugs
And killed and ate them, too!

Now, when bugs live in a basket,
Though more than it well can hold
It seems to me they had better agree..
The white, and the black, and the gold
And share what comes of the beds and the crumbs
And leave no bug in the cold!

SEVEN LITTLE PUSSY CATS
Eulalie Osgood Grover

Seven little pussy cats
          invited out to tea,
Cried: "Mother, dear, may we go,
          for good we'll surely be?
We'll hold our things
          as we've been taught
Cup in the left, spoon in the right,
          And say "only half of that"
Then go my darling pussycats,
          said the proud mother cat.

 The seven little pussy cats
          went out that night to tea
Their coats were smooth and glossy,
          and their tails were swinging free
They held their things as they'd been taught
          and tried to be polite
Cup in the left, spoon in the right,
          they made a pretty sight
But alas for manners beautiful and coats
          as soft as silk ….

The moment that the little kits
          were asked to take some milk
They dropped their spoons, forgot to bow
          and oh what do you think
They stuck their noses in their cups
          and all began to drink.
Yes, every naughty little kit
          set up a meow for more,
They knocked the teacups over
          and scampered through the door.

The Elf and the Dormouse
Oliver Herford

Under the toadstool crept a wee Elf,
Out of the rain to shelter himself.

Under the toadstool, sound asleep,
Sat a big dormouse all in a heap.

Trembled the wee Elf, frightened, and yet
Fearing to fly away lest he get wet.

To the next shelter .. maybe a mile!
Sudden the wee Elf smiled a wee smile,

Tugged 'til the toadstool toppled in two
Holding it over him gaily he flew.

Soon he was safe home dry as could be
Soon woke the Dormouse .."Good gracious me!

"Where is my toadstool?" Loud he lamented
And that's how umbrellas first were invented.

The Duel

Eugene Field

The gingham dog and the calico cat
Side by side on the table sat;
'T was half-past twelve, and (what do you think!)
Nor one nor t' other had slept a wink!
The old Dutch clock and the Chinese plate
Appeared to know as sure as fate
There was going to be a terrible spat
(I wasn't there; I simply state
What was told to me by the Chinese plate!)

The gingham dog went, "bow-wow-wow!"
And the calico cat replied, "mee-ow!"
The air was littered, an hour or so,
With bits of gingham and calico,
While the old Dutch clock in the chimney-place
Up with its hands before its face,
For it always dreaded a family row!
(Now mind: I'm only telling you
what the old Dutch clock declares is true!)

The Chinese plate looked very blue,
And wailed, "Oh, dear! What shall we do!"
But the gingham dog and the calico cat
Wallowed this way and tumbled that,
Employing every tooth and claw
In the awfullest way you ever saw..
And, oh! How the gingham and calico flew!
(Don't fancy I exaggerate ..
I got my news from the Chinese plate!)

Next morning, where the two had sat
They found no trace of dog or cat;
And some folks think unto this day
That burglars stole that pair away!
But the truth about the cat and pup
Is this: they ate each other up!
Now what do you really think of that!
(The old Dutch clock it told me so,
and that is how I came to know.)

Mr. Nobody

I know a funny little man,
As quiet as a mouse,
Who does the mischief that is done
In everybody's house.

There's no one ever sees his face
and yet we all agree
That every plate we break was cracked
By Mr. Nobody.

'Tis he who always tears our books
Who leaves our doors ajar
He pulls the bottoms from our shirts
And scatters pins afar.

That sqeaking door will always squeak
For, prithee, don't you see,
We leave the oiling to be done
By Mr. Nobody.

He puts damp wood upon the fire
That kettles cannot boil
His are the feet that bring in mud
and all the carpets soil.

The papers always are mislaid
Who had them last but he?
There's no one tosses them about ,
but Mr. Nobody.

The finger marks upon the door
by none of us are made
We never leave the blinds unclosed,
To let the curtains fade.

The ink we never spill, the boots
That lying round you see
Are not our boots .. they all belong
To Mr. Nobody!

Author unknown

Lord,

Thou knowest better than I know myself that I am growing older and will one day be old.

Keep me from the fatal habit of thinking I must say something on every subject and on every occasion.

Release me from craving to try to straighten out everyone's affairs.

Make me thoughtful but not moody; helpful but not bossy. With my vast store of wisdom, it seems a pity not to use it all, but Thou knowest Lord, that I want a few friends to the end.

Keep my mind from the recital of endless details .. give me wings to get to the point.

Seal my lips on my aches and pains. They are increasing and the love of rehearsing them is becoming sweeter as the years go by.

I dare not ask for improved memory but a growing humility and a lessening cocksureness when my memory seems to clash with the memory of others.

Teach me the glorious lesson that occasionally I may be mistaken.

Keep me reasonably sweet. I do not want to be a saint .. some of them are so hard to live with .. but a sour old person is one of the crowning works of the devil.

Give me the ability to see good things in unexpected places and talents in unexpected people. Give me the grace to tell them so.

Amen

From the Gegenheimers
(found in Healthways Magazine, Nov 1963)

Youth
Samuel Ullman

Youth is not a time of life; it is a state of mind; it is not a matter of rosy cheeks, red lips and supple knees; it is a matter of the will, a quality of the imagination, a vigor of the emotions; it is the freshness of the deep springs of life.

Youth means a temperamental predominance of courage over timidity of the appetite, for adventure over the love of ease. This often exists in a man of 60 more than a boy of 20. Nobody grows old merely by a number of years. We grow old by deserting our ideals.

Years may wrinkle the skin, but to give up enthusiasm wrinkles the soul. Worry, fear, self-distrust bows the heart and turns the spirit back to dust.

Whether 60 or 16, there is in every human being's heart the lure of wonder, the unfailing childlike appetite of what's next and the joy of the game of living. In the center of your heart and my heart there is a wireless station: so long as it receives messages of beauty, hope, cheer, courage and power from men and from the Infinite, so long are you young.

When the aerials are down, and your spirit is covered with snows of cynicism and the ice of pessimism, then you are grown old, even at 20, but as long as your aerials are up, to catch waves of optimism, there is hope you may die young at 80.

Crossing the Bar
Alfred Lord Tennyson

Sunset and evening star,
   And one clear call for me,
And may there be no moaning of the bar,
   When I put out to sea.

But such a tide as morning seem asleep,
   Too full for sound and foam,
When that which drew from out the boundless deep
   Turns again home.

Twilight and evening bell,
   And after that the dark!
And may there be no sadness of farewell,
   When I embark;

For tho' from out are borne of time and place
   The flood may bear me far,
I hope to see my Pilot face to face
   When I have crossed the bar.

Sometime at eve when the tide is low,
I will slip my mooring and sail away.
With no response to the friendly hail
Of the kindred craft in the busy bay.
In the silent hush of the twilight pale,
When the night stoops down to embrace the day,
And the voices call in the water's flow,
Sometime at eve when the tide is low
I will slip my mooring and sail away.

Through purple shadows that darkly trail
O're the ebbing tide of the unknown sea,
I will fare me away with the dip of the sail,
And the ripple of water to tell the tale
Of the lonely voyager sailing away
To mystic isles where at anchor lay
The crafts of those who have sailed before
O're the unknown sea to the unseen shore.

A few who have watched me sail away
Will miss my craft from the busy bay:
Some friendly barks that were anchored near,
Some loving friends that my heart held dear,
In silent sorrow will shed a tear,
But I shall have peacefully furled my sail
In mooring sheltered from storm or gale,
And greeted the friends who have sailed before
O're the unknown sea to the unseen shore.

Lizzie Clark Hardy

It is pagan to treat the death of a Christian loved one as if it were a loss for him or her. As a matter of fact, the word for death in the Bible signifies a move, a liberation. It means emancipation from the slavery of a physical body that is really not adequate for human aspirations. At that moment which we call death the person who inhabited that body is liberated. Loved ones who have died in Christ have never been more alive.

Richard C. Halverson
Chaplain of the US Senate
Pastor of Fourth Presbyterian, Washington DC

He Leadeth Me
Rev. John F. Chaplain

He leadeth me in pastures green?
Not always; sometimes
He who knoweth best,
In understanding kindness
Leadeth me in weary ways,
Where heavy shadows be.
Out of the sunshine, warm and soft and bright,
Out of the sunshine into the darkest night,
I oft would faint with sorrow and with fright,
Only for this... I know He holds my hand;
So whether in the green or desert land
I trust although I may not understand.

My Record by the Angels Kept.

In the book which thou art keeping,
  Tell me, angels, sweet and fair,
Have you seen my name recorded,
  On its pages anywhere?

Are there any deeds of kindness
  On the page that bears my name?
Or tell me, will its utter blankness
  Make me hang my head in shame?

Are there any deeds of valor,
  Any words of tender praise,
Any record where I aided
  Any one on life's high ways?

Are there any sacrifices,
  Sweetened with unselfishness
And little bits of color
  Caused from cheer and happiness?

Oft and oftentimes I've wondered,
  As I plod life's weary way.
If the record I am making
  Will be approved on that eternal
                                    day
—Alice M. Ban—

Handwriting above done by
Augusta (Gussie) Kikstadt, Harold's mother

Look at Me

What do you see, nurses, what do you see?
What are you thinking when you are looking at me?

A crabby old woman, not very wise,
uncertain of habit, with far-away eyes.

Who dribbles her food and makes no reply
when you say in a loud voice... "I do wish you'd try."

Who seem not to notice the things that you do
and forever is losing a stocking or shoe.

Who unresisting or not, lets you do as you will...
with bathing and feeding the long day to fill.

Is that what you are thinking, is that what you see?
Then open your eyes, nurse, you're not looking at me.

I'll tell you who I am as I sit here so still;
as I do your bidding, as I eat at your will.

I'm a small child of ten with a father and mother...
brothers and sisters, who love one another.

A young girl of sixteen with wings on her feet,
dreaming that soon now a lover she'll meet.

A bride soon, at twenty my heart gives a leap,
remembering the vows that I promised to keep.

At twenty-five now I have young of my own
who need me to build a secure, happy home.

A woman of thirty, my young now grow fast,
bound to each other with ties that should last.

At forty, my young sons have grown and are gone,
but my man's beside me to see I don't mourn.

At fifty once more babies play round my knee,
again we know children, my loved one and me.

Dark days are upon me, my husband is dead,
I look at the future, I shudder with dread.

And I think of the years
and the love that I've known.

I'm an old woman now and nature is cruel;
'tis her jest to make old age look like a fool.

The body it crumbles, grace and vigor depart,
there is now a stone where I once had a heart.

But inside this old carcass a young girl still dwells,
and now and again my battered heart swells.

I remember the joys, I remember the pain
and I'm loving and living life over again.

I think of the years all too few gone too fast,
and accept the stark fact that nothing can last.

So open your eyes, nurses, open and see...
not a crabby old woman, look closer.. see me!

Author unknown

Alzheimer's
Martha Bird (1990)

(Paul Bird speaking)
I, always so proud of my wellness
   in a cowardly fashion am slain
A sneak thief has crept up behind me
   and stolen in essence, my brain.

No chance to fight was I given
   nor know how bereft I'd become,
He, robbing by bits and pieces,
   relentless, takes all 'ere he's done.

The reins have slipped from my fingers;
   to manage, not mine anymore.
In all ways I am diminished,
   eroded, naught left as before.

But simply to say all has left me.
   is not even half of the case;
In place of my wits and my reasoning,
   an imposter is taking their place.

An imposter oft angry, demanding,
   fearful, thoughtless, or sad,
Is selfish, impatient, and stubborn ..
   all qualities I never had.

Delusive, denies and accuses ..
   such actions that I would abhor ..
Intolerant, helpless, destructive,
   in character, leaving me poor.

Though I am but one out of thousands,
   no less tragic to those I hold dear,
My crumbling world is their tragedy too.
   of whom, next, with this curse, will we hear?

(Martha speaking)
Our years were sweet without a blot
    until Paul's state had me distraught
As to my life, I've learned my lot,
I have my Paul, but have him not.

I'm Free
Linda Jo Jackson

Don't grieve for me, for now I'm free,
I'm following the path God has laid for me.
I took his hand when I heard Him call,
I turned my back and left it all.

I could not stay another day.
To laugh, to love, to work or play.
Tasks left undone must stay that way.
I found that peace at the close of the day.

If my parting has left a void,
Then fill it with remembering joys.
A friendship shared, a laugh, a kiss.
Oh yes, these things I too will miss.

Be not burdened with times of sorrow.
I wish you the sunshine of tomorrow.
My life's been full, I savored much.
Good friends, good times, a loved one's touch.

Perhaps my time seemed all too brief.
Don't lengthen it now with undue grief.
Lift up your hearts and peace to thee
God wanted me now; He set me free!

Index of Authors

Index of Titles

List of First Lines